Life

Experiences
A Poetic
Viewpoint

Life
Experiences
A Poetic
Viewpoint

*A Book of Poems
by Gary Hughes*

GARY HUGHES

Copyright © 2022 by Gary Hughes.

ISBN:	Softcover	978-1-6641-1712-9
	eBook	978-1-6641-1713-6

All rights reserved. No part of this book may be reproduced or transmitted in any form or by any means, electronic or mechanical, including photocopying, recording, or by any information storage and retrieval system, without permission in writing from the copyright owner.

Any people depicted in stock imagery provided by Getty Images are models, and such images are being used for illustrative purposes only.
Certain stock imagery © Getty Images.

Print information available on the last page.

Rev. date: 01/19/2022

To order additional copies of this book, contact:
Xlibris
UK TFN: 0800 0148620 (Toll Free inside the UK)
UK Local: (02) 0369 56328 (+44 20 3695 6328 from outside the UK)
www.Xlibrispublishing.co.uk
Orders@Xlibrispublishing.co.uk

Contents

Memories 1
The Soldier 4
Mother 6
After Love Has Gone 7
A Day At The Races 9
Depression 11
Best Friends 13
Kid's Stuff 14
Football Rivalry 15
The Euros 16
Me & Billy 18
Love Is 20
Delivery Driver 21
Absent Lovers 22
After The Passion 24
A Poem… by Lucy the Dog 25
Dreams 26
Insomnia 27
Forbidden Love 28
N.H.S. 29
Captain Tom 30
Hillsborough 31
Man's Best Friend 32
Ode to Gary Bell Snr. 33
School Reunion 34
She's All That I Want 36
Son 38
The C Word 39
Post-Traumatic Stress Disorder (P.T.S.D) 41
The Sergeant Major 43
Lest We Forget 45
Breaking Up 46
A Musical A-Z 47
Plastic Glass 49

Looking For Recommendations 50
Army Reunion 51
Sentiments From the Heart 52
New Year Resolutions 53
A New Year Toast 54
Whitby 55
A Letter To Myself 56
Final Thoughts 58

Memories

I was born and raised in the North-East.
A small mining town called Hetton-le-Hole.
The heartbeat of the place - Eppleton Colliery,
was where the men would dig for coal.

There were schools, a library and Post Office.
A church overlooked terraced streets.
The town centre was a parade of shops,
they would cater for everyone's needs.

A dozen pubs and a working man's club,
where Acts would perform on weekends.
Couples would meet up to socialise.
Enjoying great times with good friends.

Work and wages meant a happy community
but not so when the times were bleak.
The seventies brought us the miners strikes
and we were subject to a three day week.

Worse was to come some years later,
once close friends would be filled with hate,
for a colleague who dared cross the picket line
during the Thatcher and Scargill "Debate."

As kids of course, we were oblivious
to all the pains and worries in life.
That proud role of the man of the house
to provide for his children and wife.

There was plenty to keep us amused,
we were distanced from all that was bad.
An education had become a necessity,
I gave my schooling all that I had.

"You must stick in at school" I was told -
"Don't follow your Dad down the pits."
So when I qualified for Grammar School,
my Mother, she was thrilled to bits.

When I think back about entertainment,
it brings a big smile to my face -
some of the games that we played
and how things changed with such pace.

Of the gadgets you see today, there were none.
Such as laptops, X-Box or Nintendo.
We would spend hours outside playing football
or the indoor version called Subbuteo.

Whole days were spent on our pushbikes,
we were Hell's Angels, cruising the roads
or down by the beck with fishing nets,
catching sticklebacks, newts and toads.

Television was also very much different,
there were only two channels to see.
We had Grandstand as our Sky Sports
and Top of the Pops was our MTV

A young Ken Barlow on Coronation Street,
although we watched him in black & white.
The X Factor was called Opportunity Knocks,
Morecambe & Wise were our Saturday night.

That was all over forty years ago now,
some will say we were far from perfect.
But I knew then that "No" meant "No"
and all about gratitude and respect.

While the benefits of the changes in time
are there for us all to see.

I often wish I could be back there,
still innocent, youthful and carefree.

No worries about the payment of bills,
when we're old, who'll pay for our care.
Not conscious of putting on the pounds,
or searching for that next grey hair.

I think I preferred my life back then,
despite their problems, people still smiled.
If I could have my time all over again,
I would happily come back as that Child.

The Soldier

The soldier stood with his fellow men,
his training approaching its end.
Thirty one left who had passed the test,
every one of them a friend.
The parade began and the men marched by,
the trumpets playing loud.
Brothers, sisters, girlfriends, wives
and proud parents formed the crowd.

The Drill Sergeant shouts his orders
and the ranks of three obey,
moving swiftly with a swagger,
proud men they were that day.
Each one had joined so young,
not knowing what lay ahead
but it was better than the dole,
at least they'd be watered and fed.

The training would be relentless,
it had to be, of course,
taught by dedicated staff,
with an element of force.
Marching, shooting and discipline,
ironing and bulling boots
and the customary short back and sides,
shaved right down to the roots.

Camaraderie and character building
were developed as each matured,
physique and strength enhanced
by the rigorous training endured.
It was hard, it hurt and was meant to,
all part and parcel of the plan.
The process needed to accomplish
transformation from boy to man.

The parade would soon be over,
families beaming with pride.
Father and son pose for pictures,
while mothers and girlfriends cried.
A beer or two in the NAAFI
and a sarcastic raise of the glass,
for those who did not make it,
for those who could not pass.

Our soldier stood alone for a while,
passive, deep in thought.
He marvelled in his glory
and all that he'd been taught.
Who knows what would lie ahead
had he not signed that dotted line,
in and out of work perhaps,
or even a life of crime.

He was grateful to the British Army,
who allowed him to sign up that day,
to all the staff who had trained him
and sent him on his way
and for future principles and knowledge
he would gather in his stride.
All down to being a soldier,
he would tell the world with pride.

No happy or tragic ending
to the story that I tell.
Just a few words from an ageing poet
about a soldier I know so well.
Thirty five years to this very day
I set my family free
and I joined the British Army,
you see, that soldier - It was me.

Mother

Thank you for bringing me into this world,
giving me a home and a place to belong.
Teaching me good principles and manners,
showing me what was right from wrong.

For lovingly tending my cuts and bruises,
helping me to conquer all my fears.
Assuring me everything would be just fine
while carefully wiping away my tears.

Discreetly pointing me in the right direction.
Advising, agreeing with or correcting me.
Overlooking and assisting in my education,
nurturing me to the person I needed to be.

You were always there, my go to person,
with all the answers, no matter what I asked.
You were my Rock, my shoulder to cry on,
respectful, respected, beautiful and steadfast.

I'm so grateful for all that you did for me.
Through the years, the sacrifices you made.
Your patience, care and constant attention
and the overwhelming love you displayed.

You were unique and so very, very special.
If I searched the Earth I couldn't find another.
But I know if you could you would tell me
"Nonsense, I was just being a Mother."

I'll miss you forever Mam

After Love Has Gone

It had been exactly one year to the day
that he had lost his beautiful wife.
She had been the perfect mother,
his soul mate and the love of his life.
They had been together for forty years,
it was love at first sight, so they'd say
but he had never loved her as much
than the day that she passed away.

Nothing could have prepared him
for the anguish, his heartbreak and pain
and all of the words of condolence
wouldn't bring her back home again.
It was the longest twelve months of his life,
trying to adapt to living alone.
There were days he just couldn't accept,
she had gone, he was all on his own.

There were many things he struggled with,
he had questioned his faith and belief.
Why was she taken away from him?
Will there ever be an end to his grief?
It was hard to look at old photographs
or listen to certain songs on the radio
and it pained him to bump into neighbours
who found it difficult to say hello.

Occasionally he'd set the table for two,
a cup each, beside a matching plate,
nonchalantly pouring from the teapot,
not realising until it was too late.
It was comforting to hear the phone ring,
a moment that he cherished so dear,
for when the answer machine took over,
it was "her" welcoming voice he'd hear.

Their children and grandkids were amazing,
the little ones still made him smile,
watching them run around in the garden
would heal his broken heart for a while.
He often wondered if she could see them.
An Angel looking down from above.
Was it possible? Could she give him a sign?
Show him that she's sending her love.

Of course, he wasn't alone in his suffering.
Two in particular were without their Mother.
Their loss had brought them even closer,
all aware they could depend on each other.
Today they would tend to her resting place.
Together as a family - Except for One.
And remember the Lady who has been lost.
To a Husband, a Daughter and Son.

A Day At The Races

It was just after nine when they met in the pub,
for the annual trip to the races.
Big Al and Robin were the first to arrive,
followed quickly by the usual faces.
The local was soon full of budding tipsters,
some holding their Racing Post.
Pints filled the bar, with a tray of bacon sarnies -
provided by the welcoming host.

The sound of the horn and the coach had arrived,
minutes later and they're on their way.
A two hour journey to their destination,
York Races was the venue today.
Each man sat, studying the form,
sharing his views with a friend.
Crossing one out, then circling another,
till sure which to back in the end.

Three or four favourites backed to win,
maybe an outsider each way.
"Don't go crazy or chase your losses."
Wise words - the order of the day.
The general opinion was a tenner each race -
"Let's keep it all good fun"
but that soon changes with four races gone
and none of your horses have won.

A brief walk towards the Grandstand,
soaking up the atmosphere.
Stopping by one of the Guinness tents
to top up with another beer.
Some choose to join the more affluent,
in the Champagne bar close by.
With elegant ladies so beautifully dressed,
men in smart suit and tie.

A vantage point found near the winning post.
Most sought after spot on the course.
Just enough time to search the best odds
bestowed on the chosen horse.
Rows of track side bookmakers await
perched tall on wooden stools.
Lording it over their pray and thinking
"Give me your money, you fools."

The crowds roar swallows the sound of hooves
as they approach the finish line.
A photograph finish adds to the tension
with the winning distance so fine.
The tannoy announces the first race winner
to cheers from the lucky few.
Just enough time to collect the winnings
and prepare for race number two.

Six races gone by in no time at all.
Excitement from first to last
Horses and Jockeys head back to the paddocks
and punters to the Exits en masse.
The deserted race track's once green field,
littered with failed betting slips,
some of them purchased with belief and hope
and others - just dodgy tips.

Back on the coach and the long journey home,
where every race is re-run.
A pint in the local to finish the day,
in the manner that it had begun.
Those who have won will buy the drinks,
while the losers nurse their pain
but win, lose or draw, a great day was had
and next year they'll do it again.

Depression

It's one of those days that you have
when nothing seems to go right
and it's easier to just give in
than to try and put up a fight.
You've been here many times before,
in this depressive state of mind.
Dismissing their "words of wisdom"
while trying not to be unkind.

They tell you - "Look to the future"
or "try and change your ways."
"Don't worry, you'll soon snap out of it"
"It's just a passing phase."
"Come on, you know we're right"
and you nod at them and smile
but deep inside you're screaming
and you want to run a mile.

You see, unbeknown to "well-wishers,"
certain things you just can't explain.
Deepest memories of sadness and abuse
only part of what causes the pain.
Anxiety, paranoia, worthlessness and guilt,
are feelings that never go away.
There's even thoughts of ending it all
when you're having your darkest day.

On brighter days, the good times roll,
no bad thoughts to cause concern
but never distant is the knowledge
that your demons will soon return.
But you smile, put on that brave face,
it has become routine - a daily task.
No need for them to know today,
what hides behind the mask.

Depression is an invisible illness
that plays havoc with an innocent mind.
It's victims are not chosen targets
and the cause is not well defined.
We rightly mourn the demise of the famous,
this hits the rich as well as the poor.
But spare a thought for the average guy,
the one who might live next door.

Best Friends

They are one of a kind, a special breed
and always there in your hour of need.
By your side through thick and thin,
the closest thing to your next of kin.

They have your back if you're in danger,
just a phone call away, never a stranger.
Comfort and care for you, help you to heal,
can read your mind, know how you feel.

There for support when times are hard,
They'll buy you the funniest birthday card.
Laugh or cry with you, share your grief,
pay you compliments, give you self-belief.

Check out a potential boyfriend or girlfriend,
a shoulder to cry on when relationships end.
Help drown your sorrows, make it all right,
won't let you down or give up the fight.

They're loyal, dependable, reliable and kind.
Are one in a million and hard to find.
Tell them you love them, let them know.
Be sure to keep them, don't let them go.

Kid's Stuff

Some things I can recall, from being a kid,
a few distant memories and activities we did.
Just a compilation, in no order of merit,
future generations might do well to inherit.

So here we go...

Spirograph, Etch a Sketch, risk and Cluedo,
Meccano, Tiny Tears, Action Man, Subbuteo.
Sunday morning kick about - next goal to win,
hula hoops and hopscotch, with an old polish tin.
Hand me down clothes and second hand shoes.
Fish and chips wrapped in yesterday's news.
Teenage spots, nit nurse, national health glasses.
Paper rounds, bob a job, Sunday school classes.
Footballer stickers inside bubble gum packets,
platform shoes, flares and bomber jackets.
Worzel Gummidge, Stig of the Dump, The Goons,
Thursday night Top of The Pops, all the latest tunes.
Sunday night getting ready to tape the Top Forty,
standing in the corner when you've been naughty.
Cresta pop, it's frothy man. Fresh milk at the door,
Beano, Dandy, Hotspur, Diana, Shoot and Score.
Champion the wonder horse, Bonanza, scooby doo.
Grease proof toilet paper and the outside loo.
Bath night it's school tomorrow, queuing for the bus,
one hundred lines, detention, the cane, eleven plus.
Chopper bikes and clackers, homemade go karts,
boyfriends and girlfriends, first love and broken hearts.

So, there's the start to a never-ending list,
feel free to add, there'll be plenty I've missed.
Give it some thought and take your time,
here's a little help - they don't have to rhyme.

Football Rivalry

Quite a contrast for our North East fans,
as the football season ends.
Bitterest of rivals on a Saturday afternoon,
in reality, the best of friends.
Relegation again for the Red & Whites,
a second successive booby prize.
While a rally in February and March
means safety for Rafa's Magpies.

Sunderland fans will batten down the hatches,
they've lost the bragging rights.
The banter will flow North of the Tyne
from the jubilant Black & Whites.
As they travel to Liverpool and Chelsea,
they'll mock at Sunderland's agony.
With their visits to Plymouth and Walsall,
Oxford and Accrington Stanley.

But what of the future for our great teams.
Will Ashley back Benitez with millions.
A new manager is needed on Wearside and
an owner - preferably with billions.
Whatever is decided at Boardroom level,
nothing will buck the trend.
The greatest sets of supporters in the land
will follow their team to the end.

The Euros

The Euros are finally here, albeit a year late,
But fans will tell you it was well worth the wait.
Croatia were first to be put to the sword,
one nil England as Raheem Sterling scored.

Scotland were next - a tie reaped in history.
The visitors fought hard but were denied victory.
A goalless draw, much thanks to our defence,
a second clean sheet, the back line immense.

With a win and a draw the Lions have qualified,
the final group game is about places and pride.
Another Sterling goal puts paid to the Czechs.
We're into the last sixteen - Now England expects.

The old foe Germany are the next team in line.
Wembley erupts as Kane and Sterling combine.
Southgate's young guns are giving it their all,
while early favourites France and Portugal fall.

It's the Quarter Final, Ukraine are the opposition.
Our best performance yet, a four nil demolition.
Maguire and Henderson, a brace from Harry Kane,
onwards and upwards, now only four remain.

The first Semi Final and they can't be divided,
the dreaded penalty shoot out is how it's decided.
Italy win sudden death, it's they who march on.
Spain the victims - another fancied team gone.

Denmark score first but England bounce back,
as sixty thousand fans roar on every attack.
An extra time clincher means England advance.
It's been fifty five years since a Final appearance.

Two minutes in and their defence is undone.
Luke Shaw scores with a half volley on the run.
But Italy dominate, the equaliser never in doubt.
No more goals... it's another penalty shoot out.

Despite Pickford's heroics it just wasn't to be,
he saved two of theirs but we missed three.
So while the flags will be flying high in Rome,
in England - Football still hasn't come home.

Me & Billy

Me and my good friend Billy
meet up every six months or so,
for a slice of toast and a pot of tea
at this country pub that we know.

We both come armed with a list
of things to discuss and address
and for the next couple of hours
we'll sort out everyone's mess.

Brexit… Usually first on the menu
and the exploits of Boris and Farage.
The pair of them jumping a sinking ship.
If only me & Billy were in charge.

Remain, Leave, Deal or No Deal?
the four choices for Theresa May.
It would have all been done and dusted
if only She would do it Our way.

Football is next on the agenda
and making sure our team goes up.
And Southgate as manager of England?
Well - We would have won that World Cup

Then the music we hear on the radio,
well, most of them can't even sing.
We had The Stones and The Beatles
and of course Elvis Presley - The King.

I'm sure you're getting the picture -
Two old friends holding centre stage.
Contemplating anything that matters
from Donald Trump to the minimum wage.

So, just smile if you come across us
and try and keep a straight face -
It's just me and Billy on a mission
to make the world a better place.

Love Is

That feeling that you get from deep inside.
The emotion you know you just can't hide.
A passion so powerful you can't hold back.
An intensity so strong that you can't retract.
Goosebumps and butterflies rolled into one.
Kissing and dancing to your favourite song.
The pain that you get when you are apart.
The tears that you cry from a broken heart.
Precious memories you will cherish forever.
Riding the storms and growing old Together.

Delivery Driver

December - The busiest time of the year,
long days for the delivery driver man.
In to the depot early in the morning
to load all the packages into his van.
Full to the roof and front to rear,
he sets off to his destination.
North and South, East and West,
there are drivers for every location.

Endless congestion, temporary roadworks,
The traffic lights constantly on red.
Rush hour traffic and winter weather
Often hamper the journey ahead.
But he arrives on time for his first delivery,
one of seventy and sometimes more.
Down the first of many garden paths
to get the goods to the customers door.

A variety of gifts, all shapes and sizes,
pushbikes, computers, games and toys.
All eagerly received by excited parents
and quickly hidden from girls and boys.
It's cold and dark by the end of his shift
and the night time is drawing in fast.
Hungry and tired, he's heading for home,
the radio for company, heater full blast.

From the operations team and office staff,
the line workers who work night and day.
To the lorry drivers who carry the freight,
like Santa with his reindeer and sleigh.
A dedicated team providing a service,
so deliveries are made without delay
and that happy families across the land
can open their presents on Christmas day.

Absent Lovers

I sit here deep in thought, wondering what to do.
My life seems almost empty when I'm not with you.
I stare at my phone, I'm waiting for your text,
the one that lets me know, when I'll see you next.

My ringtone breaks the silence, your message, it is here,
I lovingly read your news and wipe away a tear.
Your words of warmth embrace me, always written with care,
you ask if we can meet, you know that I'll be there.

You tell me we are blessed that our love is very strong,
how good we are together, that nothing can go wrong.
We were made for one another, we are the perfect team,
have we died and gone to heaven – is this all a dream.

I come down from my pedestal, to give you my reply
but this time I won't text back, I've something else to try.
Wouldn't it be romantic if I spent a little time
to write for you a poem and send my love in rhyme.

So, I don my thinking cap
and wonder where to start,
then it strikes me as quite simple -
A message from the heart.

You bless me with a love
I have never known before,
we make love with such a passion
you leave me wanting more.

I have never known a kiss
that puts me in a trance,
the pressure of your lips,
our tongues they seem to dance.

The whiteness of your smile,
those eyes that make me sway.
Your hair, your face, your body.
So pleased God made you this way.

At times when I feel low
you tender me with care.
To you, I know I can turn,
I know you're always there.

Together our hearts are one,
our spirits they are free.
There's nothing I wouldn't do
to keep you next to me.

I love the way you love me,
your words are always true.
So darling with this poem,
I send my love to you xxx

After The Passion

I pull back the bed sheets,
wishing you were still there.
Your scent fresh on my pillow.
I find a strand of your hair.
Our time together tonight
are the thoughts within my head.
Of the passion that we shared,
when you were in my bed.
I know my dreams will be sweet,
with you fresh in my mind.
I'm drifting into sleep,
the deep and pleasant kind.

A Poem... by Lucy the Dog

My name is Lucy, that's a picture of me
I have a big sister, a cat and she is three.
You can see from my photo I'm only a pup
but I'll be big too, when I grow up.
Missy, the cat, is my very best friend
but Dad tells me I drive her round the bend.
I love humans too, there are hundreds of them
but my favourite two, are called Lucy and Ben.
Lucy is lovely, we share the same name,
she makes me laugh and we play lots of games.
Ben is so funny, he can do anything,
he comes to my house and helps me to sing.
My Dad is the best, he does everything for me,
he loves me so much, even when I'm naughty.
I couldn't be happier, so pleased he chose me,
it's just Dad, Missy and Me, our family of three.

Dreams

You came to me in my dreams last night,
an appearance so clear, I thought it was real.
It was the old you, the one I remember.
A picture of health, free from your ordeal.

It was like an old movie on fast forward,
flashbacks of happy times together.
I wished I could pause or press rewind,
desperately wanting it to last forever.

We spoke of all the good times we had,
of the present and of all things new.
You listened and occasionally smiled,
it left me thinking that you already knew.

I wondered, is there a place we go,
to watch over those we leave behind.
Maybe show a sign, or enter a dream,
try to give them that peace of mind.

I'm sure you left me with a reassurance,
that passing over wasn't to be feared.
On reflection, I wish I'd asked much more
but as in life, you faded and disappeared.

There are sceptics and those who believe.
A subject I neither contest nor defend
but certain things leave me asking,
when we are gone, is it really the end?

Insomnia

Another restless night is beckoning.
Too much going on to allow for sleep.
Can't switch off or find peace of mind.
Pills don't work and counted all the sheep.

Stress and anxiety, a head full of thoughts,
wishing these problems were only dreams.
Inwardly searching, desperate for answers.
Life isn't always quite what it seems.

In and out of bed, surfing the net.
Gate crashing chat rooms to share your plight.
The wide-awake club is buzzing as usual
but does anyone know how to win this fight?

Play relaxing music, maybe try meditation.
Kind suggestions from a new found friend.
A midnight stroll even a change of diet
but will anything bring this disorder to end.

One last glance at the bedroom clock
before daylight bursts into the room.
Kissing goodbye to the darkness of night,
the new day arriving far too soon.

Tiredness and fatigue oblivious to sound
as the pointless alarm serves its pain.
Already praying for bedtime to arrive,
knowing too well - insomnia will win again.

Forbidden Love

History may suggest it was meant to be.
They were both in relationships beyond repair.
He was lonely, just going through the motions.
She was frantic and in total despair.
They had met by chance, became good friends.
Falling in love had not been their intention,
but in each other, they found what was missing,
companionship, then love and affection.

She, had tried, but couldn't take anymore,
most weekends she was subject to his abuse.
The controlling demands, and mental torture,
always going too far, there was no excuse.
But the morning after would be all apologies,
"It won't happen again" once more he lied.
His false promises, sincerity, overwhelming.
She had likened him to a Jekyll and Hyde.

His situation different, life had become mundane,
their whole marriage had flattered to deceive.
There was no hatred and rarely did they fight
but despite lack of love, neither tried to leave.
Individual lifestyles and separate bedrooms,
there was nothing - they had drifted apart.
This new found love and desire for happiness
made him realise he needed a new start.

.

But it wouldn't be easy, families torn apart.
Questions were asked. "Did they ever care?"
The inevitable fall outs, friends taking sides.
What lay ahead for this hapless pair?
They were troubled souls, choices to make,
years gone by had seen sadness and misery.
With the journey ahead and future unclear.
Could they find strength. Follow their destiny?

N.H.S

You are life's everyday heroes,
the ones that don't wear capes.
Who provide the care and attention,
to go with our cordial and grapes.

Like the candle in a darkened room,
the calmness that eases the pain.
The treasure at the end of the rainbow
and the sunshine after the rain.

You're the silver lining of every cloud
or the shoulder on which to cry.
That light at the end of the tunnel,
or the last one to say goodbye.

Always there in our hour of need,
you're the bridge over troubled water.
A temporary replacement for a parent,
a spouse, a son or a daughter.

Our final straw, our support team,
who will never give up the fight.
The reason we stand on our doorstep
and applaud on a Thursday night.

Captain Tom

Many congratulations to you Captain Tom,
a perfect Gentleman and absolute pleasure.

As your personal marathon comes to its end.
We all salute you. Our new National Treasure

and for your gallant effort to raise many millions,
for our latest war heroes, those dressed in blue.

I quote Mr. Churchill, your once great leader.
"Never was so much owed by so many to so few!"

Hillsborough

It took twenty seven long years
for justice to come the way
of the ninety six innocent fans
who lost their lives that day.

Families dragged through courts
to fight each accusation,
finally clearing their loved ones
of this tragedy, this devastation.

Feeble apologies, too little, too late,
as the details of truth unfold.
The guilty hang their heads,
found out by the lies they told.

The healing process can begin,
respect restored to their own
and a football nation once more sing
"You'll Never Walk Alone."

Man's Best Friend

When you're ready for your final breath,
I promise you that I'll be there.
To tell you that I've always loved you
and show you how much I care.

I'll carefully remove your little collar
and cherish it forever and ever.
And as I gently stroke your tiny paws,
I'll talk of our times together.

How you'd cuddle in when I was sad,
make me smile by wagging your tail.
I was never lonely with you around,
my loyal companion, without fail.

You loved to run through fields and woods,
always checking I wasn't far away.
You filled me with such happiness and joy.
I'd never given a thought to this day.

But now we have to be strong and brave
and to banish all of our fears.
I'll be right here with you, until the end,
just try and ignore my tears.

And when you've gone to Doggy heaven,
free from all of your pain.
I'll kiss you one last time my friend.
Until we can meet again...x

Ode to Gary Bell Snr.

Friends and loved ones waited patiently,
offering comfort while sharing their grief.
The Cortege, immaculate, slowly approached.
Respectful mourners, silent in their disbelief.

The Pallbearers, tearful, enter the building,
casket draped in the colours of his team.
Closest family filled the empty pews,
followed by his friends, an endless stream.

A psalm, a daughter's poem, a son's Eulogy,
beautifully descriptive of their father's life.
Adoringly observed by the congregation,
Gary's proud children, siblings and wife.

"Have I told you lately that I loved you"
the chosen tune to send him on his way.
Prayers of concern from Reverend Newton
brought an end to proceedings that day.

Gary was renowned for his humour,
always smiling, never a frown.
His request for a funeral dress code
would soon be the talk of the town.

Ensuring he would have the last laugh
and to the Sunderland supporters' delight.
All Newcastle fans attending,
were to wear something Red & White.
........And respectfully they did.

School Reunion

A Landmark of forty years had passed,
the reunion was to mark the occasion.
The old school assembly hall was booked,
the appropriate choice, perfect location.
A mobile D.J. was set up in the corner
with a selection of music to be played,
Seventies Glam Rock and Disco,
from The Bee Gees to T. Rex and Slade.

Smiles and acknowledgements on arrival,
re-introductions to define who is who.
No embarrassment in change of appearance,
they had all put on a pound or two.
The array of characters were soon rediscovered,
the old school prankster still playing the clown
and a one-time bully, tentative in his mingling,
well aware of the occasional frown.

Two teenage sweethearts are reunited,
a little sheepish as they reminisce.
Soon laughing as they break down the barriers,
edging closer... close enough to kiss.
Silence, as an old man enters the hall,
followed swiftly by a round of applause.
He was never the most popular Teacher
but time had put paid to his flaws.

Wine and Spirits helped emotions flow,
old memories fondly discussed.
Rumours and doubts were laid to rest,
tall tales and secrets shared in trust.
Distant friendships firmly rekindled,
handshakes all round from old foes.
Phone numbers and addresses exchanged

as the evening draws to its close.
Plans for a repeat on everyone's lips
as the gathering bid their farewells.
Out of tune echoes of "We'll meet again"
as they head to their homes and hotels.
The deluge of waiting taxis depart,
ending an evening of joy and laughter.
And hopefully for some - 'New beginnings'
and not quite the end of the chapter.

She's All That I Want

She's all that I want,
sure looks the part.
Her love is real,
straight from the heart.
Some will say sexy,
others prefer class,
I say she's both,
my kind of lass.
A smile so inviting,
teeth brilliant white,
she lights up a room
like a beacon of light.
Her hair auburn red
with natural curls,
a beautiful neckline
jewelled with pearls.
Bikini girl bosom,
tort slim-line waist,
compliment dresses
of immaculate taste.
Tanned, toned legs,
one ankle with chain,
choice of heeled shoe,
anything but plain.
She's a singer of song,
both old and new.
Sit back and listen
as she entertains you.
When I first saw her move
I was put in a trance,
she was swaying those hips,
boy could she dance.
Arms wrapped around me
she'd pull me in tight,

"Rockin' and Rollin'"
well into the night.
She's one of a kind,
there's never dull days,
Yes, that's my girl,
wouldn't change her ways.

Son

I know it's your work and you have to go
but be careful out there, keep your head low.
You'll be in my thoughts each and every day.
No escaping from that, it's a Mother's way.

You cannot see the tears that I've cried
but know this my son, you fill me with pride.
It's not every boy that grows into a man,
who fights for his country in a faraway land.

A phone call, a letter, please keep in touch.
I'll miss you my darling, I love you so much.
Be sure to take care, stay safe and sound.
Counting the days till you're homeward bound.

The C Word

Two weeks of worry since my final tests
and the Doctor was confirming my fear.
His sympathetic voice explained the diagnosis
…the results that I didn't want to hear.

The disease, the illness, had took both my parents
and more recently an old family friend.
I had witnessed first-hand their suffering,
right through to the bitter end.

A numbness, disbelief, had absorbed me.
My whole body was weak with the shock.
I glanced anxiously towards my partner,
the lady who'd become my rock.

The days that followed were the toughest.
Negative thoughts had engulfed my mind.
"What have I done to deserve this?"
"Why was life being so unkind."

Despite my despair, I was surrounded by hope,
words of encouragement from those who knew.
Building me up with stories of success,
in preparation for the fight I was due.

A 'Get Well' card, a visit from a mate,
a special gift from a friend far away.
A knowing smile, a pat on the back,
all helped me to brave the day.

The love and support from all concerned
help me overcome the worst.
If the challenge ahead were a contest,
they'd make sure that I would come first.

I've gathered my strength, confidence grown,
Positivity, my first line of defence.
I'm not giving in, not ready to die...
So Cancer - Let Battle Commence.

Post-Traumatic Stress Disorder (P.T.S.D)

Three years since leaving his comfort zone,
plagued still by the things he had seen.
Proud to have served his Queen and Country
but re-living the horrors in every dream.
Gone were his comrades with their reassurance,
he'd never experienced this world before.
Nobody to turn to, abandoned and alone.
Suffering inside with his own personal war.

Doctors advised him to try group therapy,
decent people trying to offer resolution.
But his broken mind would resist all help,
for him there was only the one solution.
He strategically targeted different stores
to purchase his quota of daily drink.
Hoping to hide his obvious embarrassment
and wondering how low he could sink.

He wasn't looking for someone to blame,
although he had little respect for government.
Like a game they send troops into battle,
do as you're told - no choice, no argument.
Wealthy men of power making rich decisions,
oblivious to the outcome or consequence.
While the foot soldier bears the burden,
they lord it over their worldwide audience.

Today he had decided was to be the day,
no particular reason or special date.
Bombs and Bullets couldn't take his life,
it was the memories that sealed his fate.

Six polished medals, his regimental beret,
lay on the table by the loaded gun.
Just another tragedy, one less hapless soul.
Yet somebody's Brother, somebody's Son.

The Sergeant Major

He had watched them all grow up,
Privates, Corporals and so on.
He knew everything about them,
who was weak, who was strong.

They were nurtured and moulded together,
each with a duty to be done.
He had been their Sergeant Major
and he cared for each one like a son.

But his time in the Army was over,
twenty two years' service he'd seen.
He was saying Goodbye to his family,
the men that formed Company 'C'

The transition to civilian lifestyle
was a task in itself every day,
his heart was still in the Army,
couldn't change from his military way.

Past colleagues had kept him informed
of the call from a far away land.
His boys were going to war,
without him at the helm to command.

He had no control of the guilt he felt
and had he ever been so alone,
wishing he could be with them now
to bring them all safely home.

Devastating news from his TV screen
would echo within his head,
"We bring sad news from Afghanistan,
another British soldier is dead"

The harrowing daily updates of war.
his anger, the hurt and the pain.
His deteriorating state of mind
showed signs he was going insane.

His torment turned him to alcohol,
whiskey had become his best friend
but his tortured mind and the drink
would take its toll in the end.

The six month tour was over.
Weary men back home from their war.
But not all of them had made it,
the Company were minus four.

His body was found three days later,
hanging from the end of a rope.
No suicide note had been left
by the man who could no longer cope.

No parents or siblings were recorded,
there were no children, nor a wife.
The only words on his headstone read
…" The Army was his Life"

Lest We Forget

As a youngster I was taught in school,
about the history of conflict and war.
Years later I joined the Armed Forces,
where I witnessed and learnt much more.

Of wars, where brave men and women
fought defiantly when all seemed lost.
Heroic and victorious in their battles
…but so many paid the ultimate cost.

Survival also came at a hefty price,
many a broken heart and troubled mind.
Cruel memories and nightmares lay ahead
of the fallen comrades they left behind.

From bloodied battlefields of world wars
to the windswept deserts of Afghanistan.
We commemorate the sacrifices made
by each and every woman and man.

Every year as a nation we come together,
second Sunday in the month of November.
To pay homage to those who have died
and in silence we acknowledge and remember.

To all serving personnel past and present,
for your time served and all that you do.
From a veteran of many years standing,
I respect, honour and salute you.

Breaking Up

I so wanted this to be a Love song
but the words would have come out wrong.
The truth is, I can't do this anymore,
don't even know what we're fighting for.
When did love turn to anger and hate,
couldn't we just try to communicate.
It's not all you, we are both the same,
always trying to find a reason to blame.

Am I really that person you tear to shreds?
Thought we were Lovers, thought we were friends.
Aren't you tired of all this hurt and pain?
I haven't got the energy to try again.
There were happier times, that's for sure.
Such a pity we couldn't find a cure.
But it's over now. The end of the show.
Have to accept it, let each other go.

The heartache's not easy. The bitterest pill.
You know I love you. And I always will.
Maybe another place or another time,
things might have worked out just fine.
But there's no new tomorrow, no final dance.
We've both exhausted our "one last chance."
It's time for change. Time to move on.
Maybe one day I'll write that Love song.

A Musical A-Z

Abba gave us 'Dancing Queen' and 'Waterloo'.
A-ha said 'Take on me', Adele just 'Hello'.
B for Bee Gees, Bay City Rollers and Bowie
and The Beatles - John, Paul, George and Ringo.

Chris Rea told us all about 'The Road to Hell'
and Chuck Berry played with his 'Ding a Ling'.
While The Doors were 'Riders on the Storm'
Dire Straits were the 'Sultans of Swing'.

Ed Sheeran recalled 'The Castle on the Hill'
and Frankie 'relaxed' in Hollywood.
Fleetwood Mac brought us all 'Rumours'
Feargal Sharkey had a heart that was good.

G for George Michael, Genesis, Guns & Roses.
The Human League asked 'Don't you Want me'?
Australia gave Michael Hutchence and INXS,
James Blunt sang about a woman of beauty.

Kirsty MacColl had a hit with The Pogues,
Kate Bush moved us with 'Wuthering Heights'.
Lionel Richie was 'Dancing on the Ceiling',
Meatloaf in 'Paradise by the Dashboard Lights'.

Madonna informed us she was 'Like a Virgin',
Marley entertained with Reggae and dreadlocks.
Michael Jackson terrified us with 'Thriller'
while Neil Diamond's 'Love was on the Rocks'.

The Gallagher brothers gave the world Oasis,
Prince wanted you to bathe in 'Purple Rain'.
The Proclaimers walked 'Five Hundred Miles'.
Pink Floyd 'Comfortably Numb' with 'Arnold Layne'.

Status Quo were 'Rocking all Over the World',
Bohemian Rhapsody broke records for Queen.
R.E.M let us know that 'Everybody Hurts'
and Roxy Music had the 'Same old Scene'.

The Rolling Stones were 'Painting it Black',
Style council asked you to 'Speak like a Child'.
Snow Patrol, The Stranglers, Spandau Ballet
and 'Don't you Forget About' Simple Minds.

Tom Petty, Talk Talk and Tears for Fears.
T. Rex 'Love to Boogie' and 'Ride a White Swan'.
UB40's 'Rat in the Kitchen' with 'Red, Red Wine'.
Ultravox were in 'Vienna' and U2 gave us 'One'.

The Undertones, 'Jimmy Jimmy' 'Teenage Kicks'
The Verve talking drugs and Visage 'Fade to Grey'.
Wet Wet Wet covered 'Love is all Around'
'Won't be Fooled Again' is what The Who say.

XTC were 'Only Making Plans for Nigel'
and Yes were the 'Owners of a Lonely Heart'
Finally, Led Zeppelin and 'Stairway to Heaven'
Save the best till last - Now that's smart.

Plastic Glass

As far as new Indie bands go
Plastic Glass are one of the best.
Catch them live, you won't be disappointed.
Sunderland's very own, always pass the test.

Front man Lewis, entertainment with a smile,
Rock steady Ben, the brains and bass.
The flawless Dylan on lead guitar,
Frazer on drums, more than a pretty face.

From ballads 'For You' and 'Broken Town',
crowd favourites, 'The Game', 'What That Means',
to Anthems 'Counterweight' and "Till the End',
the new singles 'Let Me Know' and 'Come Clean'.

Glasgow, Newcastle, Manchester, Leeds.
They rock the stage wherever they play.
A must see band, get your ticket!!
Take a mate… Let them lead you astray.

Looking For Recommendations

Can anybody help me, I need new things to do.
Give me mental strength, before I go insane.
Call it self isolation or solitary confinement
but one thing is for sure, it's all a bloody pain.

I've never watched so much television
from early morning until last thing at night.
There's holiday destinations and then cookery,
sick to death of quizzes, I never get them right.

I've seen all the latest movies, up to date on soaps.
Nature shows, documentaries, news reports galore.
Watched every box set Netflix has ever shown,
comedy classics from years ago, seen them all before.

My diet is out the window, I've never been so big.
Discipline's disappeared, I eat anything resembling food.
So desperate for company I've started talking to myself,
don't mind so much but at times I can be quite rude.

I've searched the loft for old papers and magazines,
if I had a Library I would have read every book.
I now have a beard and my hair is out of control
but I've covered every mirror so God knows how I look.

Is it a Monday or a Tuesday or maybe it's weekend.
Perhaps you're like me and lost all track of time.
No matter which day it is I have to say goodbye,
Corrie is just starting and I'm out of things that rhyme.

Army Reunion

The date was set and they came in numbers
Veterans / Comrades once stationed together.
Travelling by planes, trains and automobiles,
determined to be there, no matter the weather.

July Twenty Eight, muster parade at three.
Dave Pickford's place the rendezvous.
An open field with shelter and Barbecues,
Bratties and Frikadellen on the menu.

Heartfelt embraces and firm handshakes,
as the ex-soldiers and partners mingled.
Old stories and tales spark roars of laughter
as once great friendships were rekindled.

The wind and rain couldn't stop the band,
and the girls rocked the makeshift dance floor.
Cases of beer and wine were absorbed
as the group had fun like never before.

A poignant speech and a minute's silence
for those of us who had lost their fight.
A rasping performance from our very own piper
as 'Flower of Scotland' brought end to the night.

A huge Thank You for making this happen.
Dave, Chris, your family and friends.
Many happy memories were made this day
and affirmation that - Friendship never ends

Sentiments From the Heart

Help me to learn, teach me to cope.
Keep doubt away, fill me with hope.
Love me tomorrow as much as today.
Don't ever change, keep life this way.
I'll share my heart, my body and mind.
Care for, protect you, be honest and kind.
Give all my strength, do all that's asked.
Love you each day more than the last.

New Year Resolutions

Another year will soon be upon us,
time for your new year's resolution.
Give it some thought, make it positive,
don't build barriers, find a solution.
Lose the pounds you gained at Christmas,
start that diet, maybe join the gym.
Try going on long walks, even a run,
Invest in some dumbbells, go for a swim.

Be more tidy, watch less television,
find a hobby, be happier and smile.
Appreciate others, show that you care.
Say that "I love you" once in a while.
Give up bad habits, quit the smokes,
don't drink too much, give it a rest.
Have fun, be healthy. You've only One Life,
be sure to look after it. Make it the best.

A New Year Toast

Ladies and Gentlemen please be upstanding.
Could I ask you to raise your glass?
In honour of the ones that we loved
who through the year have sadly passed.

To the Men and Women of our Armed Forces,
whose duties will never be done.
The Doctors and Nurses on the frontline,
I thank you, each and every one.

The brave policeman pounding the beat,
keeping us safe and fighting crime.
Our wonderful Ambulance and Fire crews
and the volunteers who give up their time.

Finally, as we welcome in the new year,
say goodbye to disappointment and sorrow.
Be happy, be healthy, prosperous and hopeful
and look forward to our new tomorrow.

Whitby

A warm and homely, pet friendly cottage,
the apt description from the website page.
With rural surroundings and a sea view,
most appealing to those of a certain age.
Less than two hours down the East coast
to my new home for the next week or so.
The warmest of welcomes from the hosts
and some helpful advice on places to go.

Healthy walks in the North Yorkshire moors,
beautiful beaches and Robin Hood's Bay.
A train journey across the National Park,
So much to do as I plan my week's stay.
Looking forward to a venture into Town,
from the location a pleasant walk or drive.
Recommended I should get there early,
to watch it grow and see it come alive.

The Abbey and Saint Mary's church stand proud,
above the narrow, cobbled streets of shops.
Visit the many themed pubs and bars,
frequented by vampires, ghouls and goths.
Market stalls and cafes surround the harbour,
where local boatmen offer tours and trips.
Another of the popular town's allurements -
The must try, famous fish and chips.

Neighbouring Towns offer alternate excursions.
Scarborough, Filey, Bridlington, are three.
All just a short distance down the coast,
with similar attractions by the sand and sea.
Once you've been here, you'll always return
to this picturesque town reaped in history.
Climb the hundred and ninety-nine steps
and see the beautiful views of Whitby.

A Letter To Myself

Imagine being able to go back in time,
share with yourself what you know now.
Advise on subjects that affected your life
and what to do, when, why and how.
Offering knowledge from the current day,
to your young self in the form of a letter.
Here are a few things that I might say
to try and make life a little better.

When you are small life is full of fun,
enjoy the laughter and playing the fool.
But, very important. Be ready to learn.
be sure to study and stick in at school.
Your teenage years will be the toughest,
emotionally testing, feeling so deprived.
But times were hard and Mam did her best.
Remember this and don't worry, you survived.

You will soon put all of this behind you
and realise that it was just a phase.
Your new social life is about to happen,
discovering pubs and clubs, happy days.
And when the time is right to fall in love,
don't be afraid - Your heart will know.
Your main challenge still lies ahead.
You've found the One, don't let them go.

Choose friends wisely, don't be led astray.
Stay out of trouble, don't commit crime.
Try to be patient, well-mannered and polite,
don't make assumptions, always be on time.
Be a confident person but not too ambitious.
On a lighter note, change football teams.
I'm only joking, I know it's in your blood,
so, keep the faith and follow your dreams.

There's more to come but I won't let on,
certain things you must do for yourself.
Make sure you're there to enjoy it all,
stay fit and well, look after your health.
All in all, life hasn't been too bad,
but there's room for a little nip and tuck.
Now nobody knows you as well as I do.
Look after me, be happy and Good Luck.

Final Thoughts

The old man lay in his hospital bed,
he was suffering like never before.
Just a machine to keep him alive,
the medication couldn't do anymore.
Subconsciously aware the room was full,
family members, tears in their eyes.
He knew of course of the reason.
They were there to say their goodbyes.

Deep in sleep, his life passed him by,
historic encounters pleasing his mind.
Youthful once more, cleansed of ill health,
delving deeper to see what he could find.
He was a boy again, riding his new bike
then a young man driving his first car.
Dancing to some of his favourite songs
from the jukebox at his local bar.

Meeting the girl, he would later marry
and the children they raised together,
wrapping up presents at Christmas
and holidays that lasted forever.
He remembered the joy that he felt
when their grandchildren came along
and the utter devastation that hit him
after the love of his life had passed on.

Grateful that the pain was leaving him,
fast approaching the end of his fight.
The dreams and flashbacks were weaker.
Then, suddenly - The brightest of light.
In the distance, his adoring parents,
a long time gone, yet here, full of life.
Then the vision that told him he was ready,
the outstretched hand of his wife.

Briefly, he was back in the room.
His memory, like his body, closing down.
He knew he was leaving this world
but his ashen face bore no frown.
A brave attempt at one last smile,
to show he wasn't fearful of death.
Gazing out through the open window
as the gentle breeze took his final breath.

Printed in Great Britain
by Amazon